STORE # 2675

Date: _____

ISBN# _____

TITLE _____

APPROVAL _____

LOAN _____ OWN _____

MW01138313

Pantun
Baba Chan

For my bapak Enche Pong
and my mak Bee Choo

Pantun Baba Chan

The Art and Beauty of Traditional Baba Malay Poetry

Chan Eng Thai

Translated by Chan Teck Guan / jee chan
Illustrations by Crop.sg

TUTTLE Publishing

Tokyo | Rutland, Vermont | Singapore

To Download or Stream the Free Audio Recordings:

1. Check that you have an internet connection
2. Type the URL below into your web browser:
   https://www.tuttlepublishing.com/pantun-baba-chan

For support email us at info@tuttlepublishing.com.

Contents

Foreword by G.T. Lye

AN EASILY OVERLOOKED aspect of Peranakan culture today is its literary and performance traditions that encapsulate the art forms of *pantun* writing and *dondang sayang*. In the past, performing *pantuns* to the live music of *dondang sayang* was a popular way for Peranakans to celebrate birthdays and weddings.

To excel at writing *pantun*, one needs to be witty and humorous. This is especially so when singing *dondang sayang* as *pantuns* are created spontaneously and in quick repartee with other singers.

Today, I observe that very few Peranakans can compose *pantuns*. It is difficult to encourage new generations of Peranakans to develop interest and skill in *pantun* writing due to a decline in Baba Malay speakers among Peranakan Singaporeans over the past decades. We are therefore fortunate that some continue to champion this remarkable art form. Baba Chan Eng Thai is one such person who has contributed to the revitalisation of *pantun* writing in Singapore through his exemplary and spirited work.

Congratulations Baba Chan. Your book will inspire others to follow suit so that the Baba Malay *pantun* will not be forgotten in the years to come. *Hidop lah pantun-pantun Peranakan!*

Gwee Thian Lye

Pantun-writer and Wayang Peranakan performer
Recipient of the inaugural Steward of Singapore's Intangible Cultural Heritage Award (2020), National Heritage Board
Singapore

Cuaca redup di utara,
Dudok berehat ditepi paya;
Hidop penoh dengan budaya,
Umpama pokok lebat berbuah.

Kupu-kupu terbang melayang,
Hinggap mari di pokok delima;
Rimau mati tinggalkan belang,
Manusia mati tinggalkan nama.

...

The sky darkens in the north,
Sit and rest by the marsh;
A life lived full of culture,
Is as a tree laden with fruit.

Butterflies flit and flutter by,
Landing on a pomegranate tree;
The legacy of a tiger is its stripes,
The legacy of man is one's name.

Introduction by Chan Eng Thai

THE SPRAWLING BUNGALOW at No. 40 Lorong 27A Geylang brings me back to a bygone era when extended families lived together and spoke in a common language called Baba Malay.

That bungalow belonged to my grandfather, Mr. Chan Koon Teck, who through his Will directed that the house be sold ten years after the death of his wife, my grandmother Madam Ong Chye Neo. I was born and grew up in that house, home to fifteen people across four families, until that fateful day when it was sold. Now, in its place, stands an eight-storey condominium on a road mundanely renamed Geylang East Avenue 1!

The common thread that bound the extended family members of the household of Mr. Chan Koon Teck was Baba Malay, which was used in multivarious manners throughout our daily lives. As No. 40 Lorong 27A Geylang was the *rumah abu* (ancestral home) of the Chan Family, *semayang* (rituals of ancestor veneration) and the celebration of Chinese festivals were faithfully carried out throughout the year.

The *pantuns* featured in this book pay homage to the household of that *rumah abu*. The Baba Malay employed in my *pantuns* is the language I learned and spoke in the everyday conversations and encounters with my family living in that *rumah abu*.

The other locale that nurtured my command of Baba Malay was the house at No. 30 Lorong 25A Geylang where my maternal elders not only spoke in effortless, expressive Baba Malay but also instilled in me an appreciation of Hokkien street opera! That was how I grasped the many Hokkien words and phrases throughout the Baba Malay Language. They reflect the integral Chinese elements within Baba Nyonya heritage, interwoven and amalgamated with local Malay culture and traditions.

Presently, the number of speakers of Baba Malay among the Peranakans in Singapore is dwindling and appreciation of *pantuns* in Baba Malay is but among a few. With this book, it is my sincere wish to document a part of Peranakan culture for progeny of the Peranakan community. The succinct beauty of the Baba Malay *pantun* should be preserved and highlighted as a unique expression of Peranakan culture.

I began penning *pantuns* when I was invited to emcee at a cousin's wedding dinner twenty-five years ago, during which I recited a *pantun* I composed in honour of the wedding couple. Since then, I have had the honour of writing and reciting my *pantuns* for a Thai Princess in Phuket, a Chief Minister of Penang, a Prime Minister of Singapore, three Presidents of Singapore and at numerous Baba Nyonya Conventions, school events, birthdays and funerals.

My earnest desire is for the Baba Malay language to be appreciated and for future generations of Baba Malay *pantun* writers to follow after me.

Bibik dulu suka melatah,
Baba kopiah pakay lawa;
Cakap satu dua patah,
Karang pantun budaya mewah.
…

The Bibiks' cascading speech,
A Baba impeccably dressed;
Let's start with a word or two,
Pantuns express our vibrant culture.

Baba Chan Eng Thai
18 March 2023
Singapore

Life

Bukak Pantun

Bila nio lalu pun tak sedair,
Sian pukul tambo boleh silap;
Bibik chiaogay mulot gobair,
Cherotay siang sampay gelap!

...

The matriarch passes without notice,
Even an immortal makes mistakes;
The effusive busybody bibik,
Chatters endlessly from dawn to dusk!

For the opening of the Baba Nyonya Literary Festival 2024
The National Library, Singapore
27–28 July 2024

Bahasa Baba

Pisang mas di-atas peti,
Ada dua biji bekembar;
Cakap menulis kita mesti,
Baru Hidop Bahasa Baba.

...

A comb of golden bananas,
Bear two ripening twins;
As we strive to speak and write,
Baba Malay will thrive anew.

Kueh Cuci Mulot

Gawoh tepong kueh boulu,
Gula Melaka kueh dadair;
Menantu makan Nio lalu,
Atair bawah tak sedair.

...

Flour for fluffy sponge kueh,
Palm sugar for rolled kueh;
Her mother-in-law has passed,
Yet the daughter-in-law is oblivious.

Laok Peranakan

Ikan selair sumbut cili,
Itek tim tambair brandy;
Kalu makan laok ini,
Dunia terbalik, Baba takperduli.

...

Yellowtail fish stuffed with chilli,
Brandy splashed in duck soup;
Sitting down to this splendid feast,
The Baba ignores a collapsing world.

Intan Berlian

Kerosang berlian locket intan,
Cucok sanggol mas merah;
Jari chinchin biji bintang,
Nyonya berkebaya cukop lawa.

...

Diamond-set brooch and locket,
Warm glow of golden hairpins;
Her finger a celestial gem,
Nyonya adorned in radiant kebaya.

Bulan Ramadan

Enche Wahid pergi Geylang,
Beli kain sepuloh elah,
Kedai mas nampak gelang,
Beli-kan isteri- Siti Zaleha;

Serebok kopi dari Muar,
Harum wangi sampai Sempadan,
Baba Nyonya ucapkan semua,
Selamat puasa bulan Ramadan.

...

Mr. Wahid went to Geylang,
Searching for ten yards of cloth,
He brought home a gold bracelet,
For his wife Siti Zaleha;

Ground coffee from Muar,
Its fragrance reaches Sempadan,
Babas and Nyonyas wish you,
Blessed fasting this holy month.

For The Peranakan Association Singapore
15 July 2012

Maaf Zahir dan Batin

Sultan Pahang pergi ke-Pekan,
Sambot Baginda Datuk Datin,
Hari Raya saya ucapkan,
Maaf zahir dan batin;

Nyonya buat pulot tekan,
Letak dalam kepok tin,
Hari Raya saya ucapkan,
Maaf zahir dan batin.

...

The Sultan of Pahang visits Pekan,
Celebrating the noble and beautiful,
On this auspicious day,
Forgive me inwardly and outwardly;

The Nyonya presses glutinous rice,
steamed and stored in a tin case,
At the close of this fasting month,
Forgive me inwardly and outwardly.

Pantun-pantun Nyonya Su Kim

1.

Bungah telang warna biru,
Tanda kueh apom bokkuah,
Nyonya jati rajin poonsoo,
Rumah tangga perintah semua;

Kain robia jait kebaya,
Sarong batik pakaian Nyonya,
Budaya Baba hadat kaya,
Ikut turut dewasa belia.

...

Petals of the butterfly pea flower,
Paint pancakes an azure blue,
The meticulous and talented Nyonya,
At the very helm of the family;

Fine voile for a kebaya,
The Nyonya wrapped in sarong batik,
Baba culture rich and alive,
Fostered across generations.

2.

Sulam kebaya ayam itik,
Daun pokok sama ikan,
Lukisan hidup sarong batik,
Nyonya pakai menunjukan;

Ketam batu ada tangkap,
Letak semua satu peti,
Jangan simpan saya harap,
Banyak rahsia dalam hati.

...

Chickens and ducks embroidered,
Leaves flowers fish on a kebaya,
Spirited art of sarong batik,
Worn proudly by the Nyonyas;

Mud crabs caught in a trap,
Stored safely now in a chest,
I hope you're not concealing,
Numerous secrets within you.

Pantun dua-dua dikarang untuk buku Kebaya Tales dan Sarong Secrets
dituliskan pada Nyonya Lee Su Kim
8 March 2014 农历二月初八

Satu Keretar Dua Lembu

Bunga Rose harum wangi,
Kerumun banyak tabuan lebah,
Carik perompuan siang pagi,
Gila urat betol si Inche Baba;

Dalam rumah laki kita,
Bila luar jangan cemburu,
Perkara ini orang kata,
Satu keretar dua lembu!

…

A sweet fragrant rose,
Wasps and bees swarm loudly,
Chasing skirts night and day,
A crazed lascivious Baba;

The husband is securely home,
Don't be jealous when he's out,
As the Nyonya would say,
One cart drawn by two cows!

For Nyonya Su Kim's book
Manek Mischiefs: Of Patriarchs, Playboys and Paramours
14 February 2017

Valentine's Day pulak!

Khoo Keat Siew

Pantai cantik Batu Ferringhi
Angin kencang pohon indah,
Perbuatan baik tinggi tinggi,
Hidopan Keat Siew mula ada;

Apa datang senyum ketawa,
Tulus ikhlas tua muda,
Hidopan dia sungguh mewah,
Kerendahan hati kepada semua.

...

Tranquil coasts of Batu Ferringhi,
Its trees whisper in the sea breeze,
Good deeds of every kind,
Keat Siew has fulfilled throughout life;

Greeting all things with joy,
Sincere to young and old,
A life blessed with richness,
Led with true humility of heart.

For Dato' Seri Khoo Keat Siew's book, *Rebel With A Cause*
8 May 2017

Presiden Nyonya Pertama

Keturunan Medan Khek lang,
Benih A Fei empat sigi,
Kong Ma gitu cermelang,
Cukop bangga Nya Peggy;

Ahli mayak tapi satu suara,
Kompolan kita kaya lama,
Persatuan Peranakan Singapura,
Peggy, Presiden Nyonya Pertama!

...

Descended from Medan's Khek,
Heirs of Tjong A Fie the world over,
Within a lineage of such nobility,
Nyonya Peggy is duly proud;

Many members but one voice,
A union of rich heritage,
The Peranakan Association of Singapore,
Peggy, the first Nyonya President!

In honour of Nyonya Genevieve Peggy Jeffs
1st Nyonya President, The Peranakan Association Singapore
8 February 2023

Orang Biasa

Pokok tembusu jadi alang,
Kayu balak buat jembatan;
Bila Enche suruh bikin barang,
Mana boleh taah terimakan?

...

Beams sawn from a tembusu tree,
Bridges built with sturdy logs;
Upon your summoning,
How could I turn a deaf ear?

Baba Peter Wee

1. Pantun ditulis pada Baba Clement Tan Hye San:

Baba Peter Wee turunan TiongHoa,
Chokong datang dari Negeri Cina,
Baba Wee turunan tingkat lima,
Suda jadi anak jati Baba Nyonya;

Katong Antique House shorga pada dia,
Penoh hartabenda dulu kala,
Buat tanda mata budaya Baba,
Harap kekal selama lama-nya.

…

Baba Peter Wee of mainland descent,
Ancestors hailing from China,
With five generations before him,
He was born a true Peranakan;

Katong Antique House, a paradise
Filled with storied relics,
Treasure trove of our heritage,
May it flourish into the future.

2. Pantun dibalas pada Baba Chan Eng Thai:

Turunan Tionghoa Baba Peter Wee,
Makcho nyonya chokong Cina,
Pinggan mangkok kebaya tokwee,
Katong Antique House penoh indah;

Perasan perasan barang manusia,
Di shorga tak boleh bawak dia,
Baba Wee chakap ini bukan rusia,
Tebair budi baik kekal homiah!

. . .

Baba Peter Wee of mainland descent,
Ancestors Chinese and local born,
Material culture of the Peranakans,
Fills Katong Antique House with beauty;

These mortal surroundings,
Can't be carried into the next world,
Baba Wee shares what is no secret,
Spread kindness and be forever blessed.

For the book launch of Baba Peter Wee's memoir, *A Baba Album*
17 June 2017

Makan Sampay Mabok

Sedap enak makanan Embok,
Kuah lada masak ikan pari;
Bila Baba makan itu laok,
Sampay mabok tak perduli.

. . .

Exquisite food of the ancestors,
Stingrays stewed in spicy pepper;
A Baba will eat till he's dizzy,
And carry on fully unbothered.

Masak Sampay Pengsan

Perah santan parut kelapa,
Kuah hee peow ayam pesak;
Kupas bawang tumbuk rempah,
Sampay pengsan Nyonya masak.

...

Ground coconut foamy milk,
Simmering chicken fish maw broth;
Peeled shallots in a fiery spice blend,
The Nyonya cooks relentlessly.

Makko Teck Neo

Mak masak ajair anak,
Agak agak suma boleh,
Kueh sedap laok enak,
Dapat harum ailio meleleh;

Erup kering kuah heepeo,
Cuci mulot kueh dadair,
Makan kat Makko Teck Neo,
Nio lalu pun tak sedair!

...

Imparting wisdom to her child,
The mother teaches with instinct,
Delectable kueh delightful dishes,
Fill a table of drooling guests;

Fish maw soup drunk clean dry,
Tender palm sugar coconut crepes,
Business as usual at Makko Teck Neo,
A home of irresistible cuisine!

For Nyonya Peck Teck Neo of Makko Teck Neo
4 February 2023

Festivities

Kawin Natalie & Ruben

Apom bokuah cukop pekat,
Ada pisang rajah lagi sedap,
Natalie Ruben sepasang lengket,
Jereki rahmat anak dapat;

Ada rusiah jangan simpan,
Bukak suara terus terang.
Kalu begini seluru hidopan,
Aman sentiasa suma pengann.

...

Pancakes dipped in rich sweet sauce,
Irresistible with sliced bananas,
Natalie and Ruben now enjoined,
Blessings of grace and fertility unto them;

Clear your heart of secrets,
Speak honestly with one another,
Heed this and your lives ahead,
Shall be balanced and serene.

For the traditional Peranakan Wedding of
Nyonya Natalie & Dr. Ruben
17 November 2019, Bulan Sepuloh Jee-It,
Melaka

Kasih Lima Puloh Taon

Perot lapair hari petang,
Nasi ulam berjenis daon,
Jaoh dekat semua datang,
Kasih lima puloh taon;

Ayer cincang tak boleh putus,
Api galak tak boleh padam,
Cinta Aman berjalan terus,
Satu cakap dia-tu diam.

...

Hunger in the late afternoon,
Herbal rice of assorted leaves,
From near and afar we come,
To honour your fifty years of love;

Flowing water cannot be severed,
Nor a fierce flame be doused,
Love and peace are all enduring,
When taking turns to speak and listen.

For the golden wedding anniversary of
George Chia & Chan Cheng Keow
27 December 2015

Cinta Lima Puloh Taon

Dalam taman banyak bunga
Kumbang pileh Mawar muda,
Sebab itu isteri istimewah,
Suami cinta selama lama;

Anak menantu cucu ada,
Bila bekompol senyum ketawah,
Saya doa Enche Chee keluarga,
Aman padu turunan mewah.

…

In a garden abloom with flowers,
A beetle rests on a young rose,
For his exceptional wife,
The husband's love is everlasting;

Children, in-laws and grandchildren,
Buoyant laughter at every gathering,
My heartfelt prayer for the Chee family,
Is for peace, unity and prosperity.

For the golden wedding anniversary of
Mr. & Mrs. Chee Swee Hoon
23 June 2018
Melaka

Convensi Baba Nyonya Dua Lapan

Bunga Kekhwa bunga Cempaka,
Warna hidop harum wangi,
Baba Nyonya asal Melaka,
Penduduk tanah antara negeri;

Buah Cempedak atas tinggi,
Jolok petik lapan biji,
Waktu zaman datang pergi,
Warisan Peranakan lama puji.

…

Chrysanthemum and Frangipani,
Vivid and sweetly fragrant,
The Baba Nyonyas came from Malacca,
Children of many lands;

Cempedak hang high in the trees,
Pluck eight of them with a bamboo pole,
Time passes now and then,
Peranakan culture cherished through the ages.

For the 28th Baba Nyonya Convention
hosted by The Peranakan Association Singapore
6–8 November 2015

Chetti Melaka Kota Singa

Kueh koci kueh dadu,
Pisang mas putu tegar,
Dari Tamil tanah Nadu,
Chetti Melaka Kota Singa;

Intan berlian mas suasa,
Cukop halus Nyonya Baba,
Sambot budaya antarabangsa,
Peranakan Chetti istimewa.

...

Soft light tender kueh,
Steamed bananas fragrant rice cakes,
Forebears from Tamil Nadu,
To Malacca and the lion city;

Cut diamonds glimmer of gold,
Nyonya Baba most refined,
A magnificent blend of cultures,
Found in the Peranakan Chetti.

For The Peranakan Association Singapore
at the Peranakan Indian Symposium
of the Peranakan Indian (Chetti Melaka) Association, Singapore

Asian Civilisations Museum, Singapore
4 October 2014

Terima Kasih Dato Khoo

Anak pokok tanam di taman,
Pucuk padi di tengah ladang,
Bersatu padu bertiap zaman,
Baba Nyonya mesti cemerlang;

Convensi Mula di Pulau Pinang ,
Ulang Perak Melaka di pelita,
Akal Keat Siew hati da menang,
Ribuan Terima Kasih dari kita.

. . .

A sapling planted in a garden,
Paddy stalks in a rice field,
United throughout history,
The Baba Nyonya shine brightly;

Penang's inaugural convention,
Now in Malacca twenty-five years on,
Keat Siew's idea has won our hearts,
A thousand thanks from us all.

For Dato' Seri Khoo Keat Siew
at the 25th Baba Nyonya Convention
23–25 November 2012
Melaka

Berjaya Peranakan Chetti

Kebun tanam pohon delima,
Masak pindang ikan parang,
Peranakan Chetti satu bersama,
Seni budaya selalu terang;

Gajah Berang Kampong Chetti,
Gotong royong adat kaya,
Kerejar kuat bersatu hati,
Peranakan Chetti selama berjaya!

...

Pomegranate tree in a garden,
Ikan parang in sour spiced broth,
The Peranakan Chetti altogether,
Gleaming with an illustrious culture;

Kampong Chetti in Gajah Berang,
Traditions and rites flourish in harmony,
Working and striving altogether,
The Peranakan Chetti thrive forever!

Presented to Baba Ponnosamy Kalastree,
President of the Peranakan Indian (Chetti Melaka) Association, Singapore
on the occasion of the Chetti Night
4 May 2019

Terima Kasih Presiden Halimah

Taman Istana ada buah kuini,
Harum nya wangi tahan lama,
Sungguh sibok tapi datang ke-sini,
Terima kasih Presiden Halimah;

Batik tulis dari Jawa,
Nyonya Chetti senyum ketawa,
Tidak kira bangsa satu jiwa,
Bersatu padu Singapura mewah!

...

Kuini fruits in the palace garden,
Their sweet fragrance unfading,
Joining us despite your schedule,
Thank you President Halimah;

Hand-drawn batik from Java,
Exuberant Chetti Nyonyas,
Beyond race and with one soul,
Singapore prospers in its unity.

On behalf of the Peranakan Indian (Chetti Melaka) Association, Singapore,
to Her Excellency President Halimah Yacob
6 September 2018

Puteri Sirindhorn

Bintang Timur cukup terang,
Cemelang sampai Pulau Phuket,
Puteri Sirindhorn sudah datang,
Hua hee kita se-tinggi bukit;

Kakanda baik untuk semua
Tak boleh bayar budi berat,
Doa Negeri Thai aman mewah,
Raja, Puteri panjang umor kuat sehat!

...

Bright is the Eastern star,
Its radiance reaching Phuket island,
The arrival of Princess Sirindhorn,
Brings us joy higher than mountains;

Her Royal Highness is kind to all,
Priceless is the virtue she embodies,
May Thailand be safe and prosperous,
Long live the King and Princess.

For Her Royal Highness, the Princess Maha Chakri Sirindhorn
On behalf of The Peranakan Association Singapore
at the Peranakan International Symposium, Phuket, Thailand
27–28 May 2010

Peranakan TiongHoa Indonesia

Pucok bambu dari Tiongkok,
Tanam seluruh Selatan Asia,
Siram air menjadi pokok,
Peranakan Tionghoa Indonesia;

Batik tulis Pekalongan,
Tokwi tanda lapan dewa,
Kebaya Enchim sulam tangan,
Budaya Tradisi paling mewah.

...

Bamboo saplings from China,
Taken root on a thousand isles,
Nurtured into verdant trees,
The Peranakan Chinese of Indonesia;

Hand-drawn batik from Pekalongan,
Eight Immortals on an altar cloth,
Intricately embroidered kebayas,
Revealing the richness of tradition.

For The Peranakan Association Singapore
at the 27th Baba Nyonya Convention 2014
hosted by ASPERTINA in Jakarta, Indonesia
28–30 November 2014

Seratus Dua Puloh

Assam pedas ikan kekek,
Bikin tapay pileh pulot,
Tempu macham mata kelek,
Persatuan Peranakan dah seratus dua-puloh;

Kain robia sulam kebaya,
Sarong songket kilat menang,
Budaya hadat Baba Nyonya,
Seluru dunia kasi-kan terang.

…

Tender fish tamarind broth,
Sweet potent fermented rice,
Time turns and in a flash,
The Peranakan Association is one hundred and twenty;

Kebaya of lustrous voile,
Sarong of exquisite brocade,
The Baba Nyonya cultural tradition,
Shines brightly the world over.

For the 120th Anniversary of The Peranakan Association Singapore
8 August 2020

Ulang Padri Enam Puloh

Negeri Perancis paling jauh,
Tiba Asia untuk Tuhan,
Keluar kuat sama perloh,
Kayu salip pikul tahan;

Jangot hitam sampai puteh,
Kasih beri semua ada,
Kaya miskin tidak pileh,
Sayang Padri Arro tua muda.

...

From France afar you journeyed,
To Asia for our Lord,
With hard work and sweat,
You have born many a cross;

Your beard has turned white,
We're nourished with compassion,
Treating the rich and poor alike,
The young and old love Father Arro.

For the 60th anniversary of Rev. Fr. Michael Arro's priestly ordination,
on behalf of all Peranakans of Singapore
3 July 2015

Death

Bapak Paling Sayang

Tanam padi di tengah sawah,
Beras masak menjadi nasi,
Hidopan manusia sedih kertawah,
Dapat bapak sayang baik nasib;

Makan pakay kiam kurang,
Simpan untuk anak buah,
Selamat berpisah bapak sekarang,
Berjuta kamsiah dari kita semua!

...

Rice seedlings in the wet earth,
Harvested willowed and cooked,
In life there's sadness and laughter,
I am blessed with you my beloved dad;

Thrifty and frugal in all you did,
So we can have what we have,
Today we part my dearest dad,
A millionfold thanks from us all

At the funeral service of Mr. Chan Chieu Peng, my most beloved dad,
Enche Pong (30 June 1930–13 October 2010)
17 October 2010

Mak Sayang

Mas berlian boleh beli,
Hilang Mak takleh ganti;
Ke shorga Mak dah pergi,
Doa bersama jumpa nanti.

...

Gold and diamonds are bought,
A mother is irreplaceable;
My mother has left for heaven,
I pray we meet again one day.

For my mummy, Chia Bee Choo
31 December 2020

Padri Chan Tai Koon

Mana datang ayer hujan?
Dari langgit turun bumi,
Kita datang sebab Padri Chan,
Cukop baik paling suci;

Untuk Tuhan seluru hidopan,
Balak tanggong malam pagi,
Selamat jalan ke-tempat aman,
Kita mesti jumpa lagi.

…

Where does rain come from?
Heaven falling to earth,
We are here because of Father Chan,
A kind and holy priest;

A life of devotion to God,
Bearing a heavy cross,
He has passed to another world,
Where we'll surely meet again.

At the funeral service of Fr. Alfred Chan Tai Koon
Mandai Crematorium, Hall 1
5 June 2013

Salam Berpisah

Bunga rose warna hidop,
Seleruh kebun harum wangi,
Buku dunia terakhir tutop,
Salam berpisah sakit hati;

Perkara lucu atau seksa,
Sayang Mak pasti ada,
Senyum manis sudah rasa,
Selamat jalan Ibu bonda.

…

The radiant rose shimmers,
In a garden of delicate fragrance,
Here at the final chapter,
Our parting rends my soul;

Amid delight and despair,
Your love has stayed with me,
A tender smile in a dream,
As I wave goodbye dear mum.

For dear Uncle Kip Lee, Dick, John, Peter and Andrew
in memory of Mrs. Elizabeth Lee
16 July 2015

Selamat Berpisah Jumpa Janji

Pokok Binjay tinggi tinggi,
Buah manis harum wangi,
Baik kekal seperti ini,
Itu dia Enche Kip Lee;

Bila berpisa sedih hati,
Pikay apa pasal bergini?
Satu hari bekompol lagi,
Di Syurga Tuhan janji.

...

The majestic Binjai tree,
Its fruits exuding a balmy fragrance,
Goodness flowing and abiding,
The hallmark of Mr. Kip Lee;

Sorrow at the final moment,
Wondering, why must this be?
One day we'll meet again,
In paradise, so you'll see.

In memory of Uncle Kip Lee
29 December 2018

Pantun Bukit Brown

Kopek kachang buang kulit,
Baru boleh makan biji,
Hidopan dunia mata kelek,
Beranak mati nasib janji;

Empat penjuru suma manusia,
Putus jiwa tak balik dunia,
Perkara ini bukan rusia,
Di-sini Bukit Brown akibat-nya.

...

Peel a peanut to find its seed,
Discarding skin and shell,
Life ends in the blink of an eye,
Birth and Death meet us all;

All beings from all lands,
Cease to be when life ends,
Not at all a secret,
We meet this truth at Bukit Brown.

For the Wayfinders of Bukit Brown
18 November 2017

Enche Wee Kim Wee

Orang Cina bukan Cina,
Orang Melayu bukan Melayu,
Orang apa Baba Nyonya,
Orang Singapura jorang tentu;

Raja Menteri rapat jumpa,
Orang biasa sama hormat,
Budi baik dia takan lupa,
Enche Kim Wee kepada suma.

...

They don't seem to be Chinese,
Nor can one say they're Malay,
Who are the Baba Nyonya?
Well they're Singaporeans indeed;

He's hosted royalty and officials,
Yet treats the commoner equally,
His goodness we'll never forget,
Kim Wee's legacy is for one and all.

In memory of an extraordinary and humble Baba
the late President of Singapore, Wee Kim Wee
10 February 2023

Cycles

Tikus

Beresi rumah sapu laba,
Naik teng gantong chye-kee,
Ucapkan suma nyonya baba,
Taon baru pengann hock-kee;

Lorong Stangee rumah Ba Chye,
Tak jaoh tinggal Nya Bintang,
Taon tikus kalu mo huat chye,
Buat baik jereki mesti datang.

...

Sweep the house of cobwebs,
Hang lanterns and red banners,
Wishing all Nyonyas and Babas,
A new year of peace and plenitude;

Ba Chye lives on Lorong Stangee,
Nya Bintang is not far away,
To prosper in the year of the rat,
Do good and fortune will abound.

Untuk Kompolan Peranakan Gereja Holy Family
28 January 2020
Singapura

Kerebo

Pisang tanduk buat urap,
Rebus lembut kachang kuda;
Taon kerebo kita harap,
Aman sehat tua muda.

…

Plantains and grated coconut,
Soft steamed chickpeas;
In this year of the ox we pray,
For peace and good health to all.

Harimo

Harimo raja seluruh binatang,
Mata-nya tajam badan-nya kuat;
Ini taon mayak jereki akan datang,
Apa apa bikin semua mesti huat!

...

King of the animal realm,
A tiger is sharp and strong;
Good fortune awaits you this year,
May all your endeavours succeed!

Kuching Belanda

Kuching ada berjenis jenis,
Bukan kuching tapi belanda;
Taon ini akibat semua manis,
Jereki sehat berturut anda.

. . .

There are all kinds of cats,
Oh but this one is a rabbit;
May all rewards this year be sweet,
Good fortune and health throughout.

Naga

Cuaca terang pokok berbunga,
Bulan pertama hari baik,
Taon naga rumah tanggah,
Selamat mak-bapak adek-beradek;

Chyekee merah di-atas pintu,
Makan kueh-kueh jangan malu,
Panjang umor kuat sehat tentu,
Sambot tua muda taon baru.

…

The sky shimmers over flowering trees,
A good day on the first month,
At home in the year of the dragon,
Honour and respect one's family;

A red banner above the doorway,
Help yourself to the delicious kueh,
Longevity and good health,
To one and all in the new year.

Ular

Kebaya sulam sarong batik,
Baju lokcuan seluar songket,
Taon baru pakaiyan cantik,
Ular datang si naga balek;

Kueh bangkit kueh koya,
Isi botol sampay muat,
Jereki masuk penoh kaya,
Doa bikinan semua huat.

...

Embroidered kebayas sarong batik,
Mandarin jackets silken pants,
Impeccably dressed for the new year,
Dragon is gone and snake is here;

Coconut and green bean cookies,
Fill bottles to the brim,
May we be blessed and flourish,
In all that lies ahead.

Kuda

Baba Hock pergi ke-kota,
Suka beli kueh kara,
Ini taon baru kuda,
Doa baik semua pekara;

Chayit pagi bukak pintu,
Sambot jereki sepuloh jari,
Kalau hati chengsim tentu,
Tuan-allah popi hari-hari.

...

Baba Hock heads into town,
For his favourite crispy kueh,
In this year of the horse,
May we be blessed with success;

Gates thrown open on the first day,
Palms clasped in prayer,
The pure of heart will be embraced,
In God's unfaltering grace.

Kambing

Cukop hebat pokok belimbing,
Bikin petai sambal udang,
Taon baru taon kambing,
Pekara baik mesti datang;

Satu taon satu sekali,
Bekompol kita gereja sini,
Doa Tuhan chengsim hati,
Semua pengann tiap hari.

. . .

The sublime belimbing tree,
Fried petai with sambal prawns,
This year of the goat,
Will surely greet us with joy;

At the turn of each year,
We gather in this church,
Praying to God for peace,
And harmony for all our days.

Monyet

Parot kelapa perah santan,
Gaoh tepong bikin kueh,
Monyet lompat dari selatan,
Ini taon semua siopuey;

Naik teng gantong chyekee,
Chuey it pagi bukak pintu,
Dua tangan sambot jereki,
Anak-beranak chuchu menantu.

. . .

Coconut shavings coconut milk,
Mixed with flour for kueh,
A monkey springs from the south,
Bringing success this new year;

Hang lanterns and red banners,
Gates open on the first morning,
Hands clasped in prayer,
That fortune may visit the family.

Ayam

Kayu jati bikin papan,
Budi baik jangan hutang,
Pagi bukak pintu depan,
Ayam bekokok jereki datang;

Kueh bangkit kueh koya,
Dalam kotak kueh belanda,
Taon baru baikan kaya,
Kuat sehat suma ada.

...

Planks sawn from dark teak,
Kindness without expectations,
Opening the front gate at dawn,
The cock's crow welcomes fortune;

Coconut and green pea cookies,
A box of love letter crepes,
Overflowing goodness,
Health and vigor this new year.

Anjing

Naik teng gantong chyekee,
Pasang lilin terang rumah,
Bukak tangan sambot jereki,
Chueh It sojah kongkong mama;

Kueh koci kueh dadair,
Kelapa santan gula melaka,
Anjing teriak kasi sedair,
Taon baru depan mungka.

…

Raise lanterns and red banners,
The house awash in candleglow,
Receive fortune with open hands,
Bow to one's elders on the first;

Wrapped kueh rolled kueh,
Coconut milk and palm sugar,
The dog's bark awakens all,
To the new year before us.

Untuk Kompolan Peranakan Gereja Holy Family
5 February 2018

Babi

Hati bungkus sama luak chye,
Pongtey ada rebong kantang,
Taon babi suma huatchye,
Lama keluar baru datang;

Kueh bangkit kueh koya,
Perah santan kelapa muda,
Taon baru jereki kaya,
Keluagar pengann suma ada.

…

Liver balls with fermented vegetables,
Stewed pork, bamboo shoots, potatoes,
A prosperous new year to one and all,
Out with the old and in with the new;

Coconut and green pea cookies,
Freshly squeezed coconut milk,
Abundant blessings this new year,
Peace and harmony in the family.

Untuk Kompolan Peranakan Gereja Holy Family
4 February 2019

Birth

Seh Jit Lima Puloh Enche Benjamin Seck

Nasi ulam berjenis daon,
Manis betol kueh kachang,
Sehjit lima puloh taon,
Doa sehat umor panjang;

Pergi sawah tanam padi,
Cukop lemak kuah santan.
Suma huat buat terjadi,
Mintak jereki besar lautan.

...

Rice tossed in fragrant herbs,
Fresh sweet peanut pancakes,
On your fiftieth birthday,
I wish you health and longevity;

Planting rice in the paddy field,
Full and flavourful coconut milk,
May you succeed in all you do,
Buoyed by a sea of providence.

For Enche Benjamin Seck's 50th Birthday
9 April 2023

Lima Lima Jereki Delima

Ini taon dah lima lima,
Jereki ribuan biji delima,
Badan sehat kuat sama,
Doa saya se-lama lama;

Kawan baik bintang terang,
Siang malam hati bimbang,
Berlian intan dapat jarang,
Seperti Enche ini orang!

...

At fifty-five this year,
You are innumerably blessed,
Health and strength always,
Is my sincere wish for you;

A friend bright as starlight,
I treasure dearly in my heart,
As it is with rare diamonds,
Such a person is beyond compare!

———————————
For Enche Peter Lee Peng Eng
on his Sehjit Lima Puloh Lima Taon
29 December 2018

Enam Dua

Pergi kota hari petang,
Beli mas mesti timbang,
Enam dua sudah datang,
Lagi muda jangan bimbang;

Banyak biji buah delima,
Cukop manis tidak kelat,
Doa baik selama lama,
Panjang umor badan sehat.

...

An afternoon trip into town,
Balancing gold on a scale,
Now arriving at sixty-two,
A youthful and carefree number;

Pomegranate seeds aplenty,
Each one sweet and bright,
Blessings of goodness upon you,
For a long healthy life ahead.

For Eric Michael Oey on his 62nd birthday
29 March 2016

Lapan Puloh Enche Thai Ho

Atas pintu gantong chye kee,
Seh Jit makan telor mee suah,
Dah lapan puloh suka hati,
Tunjuk gigi senyum ketawa;

Betol manis si buah kuini,
Kacang gula kueh makmur,
Doa Enche Thai Ho tiap hari,
Badan sehat panjang umor.

…

Red banners upon the gate,
Birthday noodles and boiled eggs,
Overjoyed at your eightieth,
Smiles and laughter all around;

Sweet and luscious kuini,
Flaky sugared peanut pastry,
Our prayer is for you to enjoy,
A long and healthy life.

For the 80th Birthday of Mr. Chan Thai Ho
18 December 2015

Lapan Puloh Enche Pong

Pasir Panjang pantai cantik,
Dapat pancing ikan kembong,
Wak Lenggang jaga anak Koon Teck,
Suka pukul tambor namakan Pong;

Tiah besair ada suara seruni,
Gantong chye kee sambot jereki ,
Kam siah Tuan Puan datang ke-sini,
Panjang umor mesti jumpa lagi.

…

Charming shoreline of Pasir Panjang,
Fishing lines cast for kembong,
Wak Lenggang nanny to Koon Teck's son,
Named 'Pong' for his love of the drum;

Seruni blaring in the ancestral hall,
Red banners celebrating fortune,
Thank you for being here tonight,
Live well and till we meet again.

For the Seh Jit Lapan Puloh Taon of Mr. Chan Chieu Peng
26 June 2010

Lapan Puloh Padri Arro

Roti Perancis makan mentega,
Cukop lazat minum kopi,
Untuk Tuhan tinggal keluagar,
Mimpi jadikan kenyataan hati;

Kechik besar sama tua muda,
Padri Arro gerejar-nya permata,
Lapan puloh tahun hari-ni tiba,
Lebeh seratus tahun doa kita.

...

Sliced butter on French loaf,
Delectable with some coffee,
He left his family for God,
To realise a profound plan;

Young and old, one and all,
Hold Father Arro in grand regard,
Today he turns eighty years,
We pray he lives plenty more.

For the 80th birthday of Rev. Fr. Michael Arro MEP
9 July 2011

Lapan Puloh G.T. Lye

Dulu pangong wayang ada Khairuddin,
Waris wayang Peranakan, Inche GT Lye,
Dondang Sayang dulu ada Pak Nordin,
Suara merdu sekarang Gwee Thian Lye;

Melaka asal Nyonya Baba,
Sejarah Peranakan kaya mewah,
Lapan puloh ucapkan muhibah,
Umor panjang jereki murah.

...

Khairuddin once ruled the stage,
GT Lye is his heir apparent,
Pak Nordin master of Dondang Sayang,
Gwee Thian Lye's voice rings bright today;

Baba Nyonya birthed in Malacca,
Vibrant legacy of the Peranakans,
On your eightieth I wish you,
A long life blessed with abundance.

Untuk Sehjit 80 Enche Henry Gwee Thian Lye
27 October 2018

Sembilan Puloh Dick Chia Peng Hoe

Sikit cakap sama baik hati,
Buruk bagus dia tahan,
Ba Dick sembilan puloh hari jadi,
Suma huahee puji Tuhan;

Anak Chuchu sayang suma ada,
Bini dia Chiantek si Tnglang,
Sedara kawan mintak doa,
Sehjit seratus mesti datang!

…

Unassuming with a heart of gold,
He's stood through thick and thin,
Honouring Ba Dick's ninetieth birthday,
We give joyful thanks to God;

Loved by children and grandchildren,
A beautiful gracious wife Chiantek,
Friends and family all look forward,
To the hundredth birthday party!

For the 90th birthday of Kuku Ba Dick
22 May 2022

Seratus Tahun Wee Hian Chai

Baju Cina enam butang,
Merah hidup buah angkee,
Jauh dekat kita datang,
Ucapkan pengann hockkee;

Bapak, Kong, Kongcho jadi,
Anak, soon, chitchit pun ada,
Seratus tahun hari ini,
Tambah seratus kita doa!

...

Six buttons on a mandarin jacket,
The persimmon gleams ruby red,
We've all arrived near and far,
To wish you peace and fortune;

Dad, grand and great-grandpa,
A happy lineage surrounds you,
You've arrived at one hundred,
We pray for a hundred more!

For Kukong Wee Hian Chai's 100th birthday
19 August 2023

Seratus Tahun Lee Hong Keow

Bunga melor harum wangi,
Cucuk sanggul cantik s'kali,
Dekat jauh datang ke-sini,
Sambut sehjit chin hock-kee;

Mak, Ah Mah Ah Chor jadi,
Anak soon chitchit ada,
Hari ini seratus terjadi,
Lebeh seratus doa semua.

...

Sweet-scented jasmine blooms,
Perch pierced atop a bun,
Gathered today from near and far,
In celebration of your birthday;

Mum, grand and great-grandma,
A happy lineage surrounds you,
Now at one hundred years,
We wish you a long happy life.

Recited by Dato' Seri Khoo Keat Siew on the 100th Birthday of the Matriarch
Mrs. Ong Ewe Hin, nee Madam Lee Hong Keow
19 February 2011
Penang

Membalas WhatsApp Sama G.T. Lye

Achar

CET:

Ada barang kita kongsi,
Ramay betol di pekan;
Itu achar saya kasi,
Jangan hiam bila makan!

…

We share what we have,
The town buzzes with activity;
Enjoy those pickles I gave you,
Without a word of criticism!

G.T. Lye:

Beras dari Berastagi,
Dijual orang di pasar pekan;
Itu acar kalu tuan tak kasi,
Ini tahun gua tak dapat makan.

...

Rice from Berastagi,
Sold in the town market;
If not for this gift of pickles,
I would have had none this year.

Satu Borang

CET:

Tepi pagar tanam buah paya,
Sarang burong di-atas genting;
Besok datang melawat saya,
Apa pasal yaukin penting?

...

A papaya tree by the fence,
Bird's nest on the roof;
You're coming to visit tomorrow,
What's the urgent matter?

G.T. Lye:

Ada budak fael garang,
Ada pulak fael genit;
Cuma mau isi satu borang,
Boleh di-selesai dalam lima minit!

…

Some children are aggressive,
While others are affectionate;
I just need to fill out a form,
Which can be done in five minutes!

Popiah

CET:

Wayang Peranakan paling chootmiah,
Tukang masak nomber satu;
Dengair Enche nya popiah,
Tak sedair pun bila nio lalu!

...

Star of the Peranakan stage,
First and finest among chefs,
Once I heard you're making Popiah,
Nothing else matters anymore!

G.T. Lye:

Tamba miyak pasang pelita,
Tarok mari di-tepi pintu;
Dari mana dapat cerita?
Jangan dengair semua falsu!

...

Pour oil for the lamp,
Come put it by the door;
Where did you hear such stories?
Don't listen to these fables!

Lama Tak Dengair

G.T. Lye:

Burong Tiong terebang tinggi,
Rehat makan buah nanair;
Kemana Enche sudah pergi?
Bergitu lama tak dengair.

...

A hill mynah soars above,
Descending briefly for pineapple;
Where have you gone recently?
Haven't heard from you in a while.

CET:

Rumah besar banyak bilik,
Tembok semua warna biru;
Bila Enche ke-tanah balik,
Sambot taon monyet baru?

...

A mansion of many rooms,
Walls painted a brilliant blue;
When are you returning home,
To celebrate the year of the monkey?

G.T. Lye:

Pasang pelita di-depan bilik,
Jangan lupa tukar sumbu;
Saya memang sudah balik,
Kalau tak salah sudah seminggu!

...

An oil lamp in the doorway,
Don't forget to change the wick;
Unless I'm mistaken,
It's been a week since I've returned!

Buku Pusaka

CET:

Buku Panton dulu kala,
Karangkan itu berlian mutiara;
Baba GT beri kan saya,
Kam siah Tok Guru mulia!

...

This old book of poems,
Is a work of diamonds and pearls;
Given to me by Baba GT,
Thank you esteemed teacher!

G.T. Lye:

Pokok mengkudu dari Pekan,
Sedap di ulam gulai pari;
Buku pusaka di-kasi kan,
Untuk kenangkan esok nanti.

...

The noni from Pekan,
Delicious in spicy skate stew;
This treasure I gifted,
Will remind you of me.

CET:

Kachang botol buat ulam,
Pileh pulot bikin inti;
Esok nanti itu macham,
Bila dengair sayup hati!

...

Winged beans sambal prawns,
Pick grains for steamed rice;
What will tomorrow bring?
I tremble at the thought!

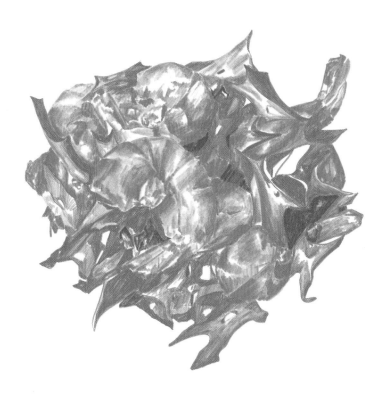

Kenny Chan

G.T. Lye:

Ayam ketupat di kota Acheh,
Daun kelapa taah lidi;
Dapat khabair sangat sedih,
Kenny Chan Melaka taah lagi!

...

Chicken rice cakes in Aceh,
The coconut leaf is boneless;
I've received tragic news,
Kenny Chan of Melaka has passed!

CET:

Pokok serunai bunga melati,
Daun kelapa taah lidi;
Bila orang sudah mati,
Jangan lupa dia punya budi.

...

Sea daisy and jasmine flower,
The coconut leaf is boneless;
When a person has passed,
Let's not forget their kindness.

Nasi Ulam

CET:

Negri Sembilan kota Gemenche,
Persiang taugay bikin mee siam;
Nasi ulam saya beri Enche,
Harap makan jangan hiam!

...

The city of Gemeche in Negri Sembilan,
Pluck bean sprouts to make mee siam;
I hope the herbal rice I made,
Is eaten without any criticism!

G.T. Lye:

Bukan garam tapi ragi,
Buat tapay sedap sekali;
Kalu hiam mesti rugi,
Ini malam dinner gua free.

...

Not salt but yeast,
To make delicious fermented rice;
It's my loss if I'm critical,
As my dinner tonight is free.

Kurang Sehat

G.T. Lye:

Pergi ke hulu tiga sahabat,
Hendak mencari burong pelatok;
Tiga minggu kurang sehat,
Baru semboh dari batuk.

...

Three friends went into the bush,
In search of a woodpecker;
After three weeks of illness,
I've just recovered from a cough.

CET:

Pisang mas pisang berangan,
Ada ditanam di Gunung Tahan;
Bahaya dah-lepas kuatay jangan,
Sekarang sihat syukur Tuhan.

...

Golden and red bananas,
Growing on Mount Tahan;
What a relief the threat has passed,
Thank God you're healthy now.

Sehjit

CET:

Bawak mangkok kat chimchey,
Cepat kering sungguh basar;
Chiah kita sehjit Enche,
Ada hati ribuan kamsiah!

…

Bring the bowls to the airwell,
Dry them off after rinsing;
A thousand thanks for inviting us,
To your birthday celebration!

G.T. Lye:

Gauh pulot uli-uli,
Gelek jadi kue ee;
Makan saja setaon sekali,
Hari besair ni rasa hua hee.

. . .

Mix rice flour and gently knead,
For glutinous rice balls in syrup;
Eaten just once a year,
On this joyous special day.

CET:

Petik kebun buah manggis,
Pergi jual Kampong Ulu;
Makan kuih ee lemak manis,
Kelek mata nanti taon baru.

...

Mangosteens from the garden,
Plucked and sold in Kampong Ulu;
Eating sweet glutinous rice balls,
The new year will soon be upon us.

G.T. Lye:

Malam nyantok cari bantal,
Tidur lelak sampay pagi;
Selamat nyambut hari Natal,
Taon baru bawa jerki.

. . .

Searching for a pillow in the night,
Sleep gently into the morning;
Yuletide blessings,
May the new year bring goodness.

Malam Pantun

CET:

Enche Johari Puan Zaitun,
Daun talas daun selaseh;
Itu malam kita balas pantun,
Saya ucapkan terima kasih.

...

Mr. Johari and Miss Zaitun,
Taro and basil leaves;
For that evening of poetic repartee,
I express my sincere gratitude.

G.T. Lye:

Kambing di-kandang kambing ke-miri,
Di-kasi makan pucuk ubi;
Kamsiah jugak saya mo beri,
Lain kali chiah-lah lagi!

...

Sheep and goats in a stall,
Fed with cassava shoots;
Once again I send my thanks,
Looking forward to the next time!

Sibok

G.T. Lye:

Dari Pekan pergi ke Muara,
Jangan lupa singgah di Ulu;
Kenapa Tuan senyap tak bersuara,
Saya sentiasa menanggong rindu.

…

Journeying from Pekan to Muara,
Don't forget to stop by Ulu;
Why have you been so quiet?
I'm anxious to hear from you.

CET:

Panggong Bangsawan di Singapura,
Dulu chootmiah Mistijah;
Bukan saya tak bersuara,
Ada sibok sama kerejar.

...

On the Bangsawan stage in Singapore,
Mistijah was the leading act;
It's not that I'm being aloof,
I've been kept busy with work.

Hari Merdeka

CET:

Beli keluak di pasar Tekka,
Masak ikan gulai peria;
Hari kebangsaan hari merdeka,
Rakyat sambut gembira meriah.

…

Pangium seeds from Tekka market,
Aromatic bittergourd fish curry;
Independence was declared today,
The people are greeted with joy.

G.T. Lye:

Kueh kochi kueh dadu,
Lain rasa mentega keju;
Hari kebangsaan rakyat bersatu,
Negara sentiasa selalu maju.

...

Kueh kochi kueh dadu,
Distinct from butter and cheese;
The people are united as one,
The country keeps forging ahead.

CET:

Buah langsat buah duku,
Pagi beli dari pasar Tekka;
Negeri aman bersatu padu,
Ucapkan selamat hari merdeka.

...

Langsat and duku fruit,
Fresh from Tekka market this morning;
A peaceful and harmonious nation,
On this independence day.

Ngkoh Thai Ho

G.T. Lye:

Pokok Pinang daun upeh,
Jatoh sebatang batu bata;
Lagi satu khabair sedih,
Ngkoh Thai Ho sudah takda.

…

A betel nut tree and its leaves,
Collapsed heavy as a brick;
Another piece of painful news,
Brother Thai Ho is gone.

CET:

Daun upeh pokok pinang,
Harum wangi bunga melati;
Orang halus tidak hilang,
Kita ingat didalam hati.

. . .

Betel nut leaves and its tree,
The deep fragrance of jasmine;
A person's soul is eternal,
We hold him dearly in our hearts.

Takut Covid

CET:

Ayer surut korek siput,
Cherimin jatoh mesti merekah;
Tuasehjit orang dah jemput,
Enche jadi pergi Melaka?

...

Digging for clams at low tide,
A mirror cracks when it falls;
We've been invited to a birthday,
Are you going to Malacca?

G.T. Lye:

Turun ke sawah pagi-pagi,
Inggin mo tuai si merah padi;
Niat memang mo pergi,
Takut Covid cancel tak jadi.

...

Descending to the fields at dawn,
Looking to harvest red rice;
I had every intention to go,
But I'm scared of Covid so won't.

Sangsara

G.T. Lye:

Pisang kaki buah angki,
Pokok tumboh tepi paga;
Banting tulang setengah mati,
Carek nafkah penoh sangsara.

...

Banana stalks and persimmons,
Their trees growing by a fence;
Broken bones and a fading life,
Full of poverty and suffering.

CET:

Piaktu tahan kayu jati,
Kapur sireh buah pinang;
Pikul balak kita mesti,
Orang kaya senang lenang.

...

A sturdy teak wall-cabinet,
Slaked lime rolled with betel nut;
We carry our burdens in life,
While the rich saunter carefree.

Syukur

G.T. Lye:

Jatoh ke tanah sebiji kelapa,
Untong sekali tak timpa orang;
Dah lama kita tak jumpa,
Apa khabar Enche Chan s'krang?

...

A coconut falls from above,
Thankfully no one was hit;
It's been a while since we met,
How's Mr. Chan doing these days?

CET:

Sebiji kelapa jatoh ke-tanah,
Parot kan bikin pulot intee;
Saya baik ada hati tanya,
Syukur betol kawan baik ini.

...

A coconut fell to the ground,
Grate it to make pulot intee;
All is well thanks for asking,
How grateful I am for a friend like you.

Afterword

Reading my dad's *pantuns* for this book has been an uncanny exercise of memory. I attended many of the events and know most of the people these *pantuns* commemorate. Each *pantun* returns me to those events and people.

Moving through these layers of memory is a chaotic yet tender affair. The smell of monsoon rain, me as a teenager in an ill-fitting shirt at someone's wedding, peeking into the dim kitchen where I find mama peeling prawns (*laksa* tonight!), the taste of fresh oily *lor bak* in a Georgetown kopitiam, treading gingerly through dense clusters of gravestones on Bukit Brown, the freezing air-conditioning of Holy Family Church, Katong. These *pantuns* are portals into worlds unto themselves, each one rising from the horizon of a language so intimately familiar to me—one which I hear only at home or the occasional community gathering. Now that many of my elders have passed on, I mainly have contact with Baba Malay through my dad. Non-standard languages have been subjected to intense marginalisation in Singapore and I often come across people who refer to Baba Malay as a "dying language".

Editing and translating this book with my dad has helped me realise how grateful I am to have inherited this incredible language—and with that, vast cultural traditions—from him. Only in the face of serious political, economic or social pressures do people stop passing on their mother tongues to their children. In Singapore today, there are an estimated one thousand native speakers of Baba Malay, most of whom are concentrated among older generations. In my view, the aim of this book is to enable a deeper appreciation of not just Peranakan culture but of how important language is as an aspect of any culture.

Actively preserving and encouraging the Baba Malay language allows future generations to access entire lifeworlds of cultural knowledge that challenge traditionally fixed boundaries of race, ethnicity and nationality.

I am immensely proud of my dad. He inspires me to be curious, humble and kind. It has been a truly special experience and my great privilege to have worked on this book together with him.

Daon kesom ikan terubok,
Nasi puteh sambal belachan;
Cakaplah bahasa embok-embok,
Budaya Peranakan lama tahan.

…

Kesom leaf with terubok fish,
White rice and sambal belachan;
Speaking the language of our ancestors,
Peranakan culture endures ahead.

Chan Teck Guan / jee chan

1 August 2024
Berlin

Acknowledgements

A big *kamsiah* to:

Susan Thin Foong for her constant presence and reminders to get this *buku pantun* published.

Daniel Teck Kian and Natasha Raj for believing in me.

Egan Teck Guan (jee chan) for the countless hours conceptualizing, translating, editing and video calling over many seas and time zones.

Zachary Chan and Nai Iyn Huii for your vision and beautiful designs.

Members of the Peranakan Association Singapore, notably, the association's past presidents, Enche Lee Kip Lee, Enche Peter Wee, Enche Colin Chee and the current president, Nya Peggy Jeffs. Along with Enche Kalastree Ponosamy, president of the Association of Chetti Melaka (Peranakan Indian), Singapore, for providing me numerous platforms to recite my *pantuns*.

My *kawans* in the Peranakan Voices with whom I sing *lagu-lagu Peranakan*, for the music and camaraderie.

Carol Chan Eng Geok for speaking a lifetime of Baba Malay with me.

My paternal family who raised me at No. 40 Lorong 27A, Geylang.

My maternal family who loved me from No. 30 Lorong 25A, Geylang.

My *pantun* and *dondang sayang* partner, Enche Gwee Thian Lye who continues to send me *pantuns* on WhatsApp, for your stories and friendship.

Eric Oey for your encouragement and giving me the confidence to publish.

All the Baba Nyonyas in Singapore, Melaka and beyond who speak the full spectrum of Baba Malay from *halus* to *kasar*, for tending to this living language.

Isi kepiting bikin bakwan,
Ayam masak curry korma;
Saya ucapkan sedara kawan,
Ribuan kamsiah satu suma.

…

Fleshy crabs rolled in meatballs,
Chicken braised curry korma;
To my dear family and friends,
A thousand heartfelt thanks.

Childhood Photos

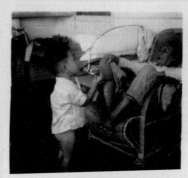

"Books to Span the East and West"

Tuttle Publishing was founded in 1832 in the small New England town of Rutland, Vermont [USA]. Our core values remain as strong today as they were then—to publish best-in-class books which bring people together one page at a time. In 1948, we established a publishing outpost in Japan—and Tuttle is now a leader in publishing English-language books about the arts, languages and cultures of Asia. The world has become a much smaller place today and Asia's economic and cultural influence has grown. Yet the need for meaningful dialogue and information about this diverse region has never been greater. Over the past seven decades, Tuttle has published thousands of books on subjects ranging from martial arts and paper crafts to language learning and literature—and our talented authors, illustrators, designers and photographers have won many prestigious awards. We welcome you to explore the wealth of information available on Asia at **www.tuttlepublishing.com**.

Published by Tuttle Publishing, an imprint of Periplus Editions (HK) Ltd.

www.tuttlepublishing.com

Copyright © 2025 Chan Eng Thai
Editor & Translator © Chan Teck Guan Egan (jee chan)
Cover Design & Illustrations © Crop.sg
Supported by National Arts Council, Singapore

ISBN: 978-0-8048-5837-3

Library of Congress Cataloging-in Publication Data is in process.

Distributed by

North America, Latin America & Europe
Tuttle Publishing
364 Innovation Drive,
North Clarendon
VT 05759-9436, USA
Tel: 1 (802) 773 8930
Fax: 1 (802) 773 6993
info@tuttlepublishing.com
www.tuttlepublishing.com

Asia Pacific
Berkeley Books Pte. Ltd.
3 Kallang Sector #04-01
Singapore 349278
Tel: (65) 67412178
Fax: (65) 67412179
inquiries@periplus.com.sg
www.tuttlepublishing.com

28 27 26 25   5 4 3 2 1
Printed in China   2502CM

TUTTLE PUBLISHING® is a registered trademark of Tuttle Publishing,
a division of Periplus Editions (HK) Ltd.